PROTECTING WILDLIFE

Malcolm Penny

Conserving Our World

Acid Rain
Conserving Rainforests
Waste and Recycling
Conserving the Atmosphere
Protecting Wildlife
The Spread of Deserts
Farming and the Environment
Protecting the Oceans
Conserving the Polar Regions

Cover: The cheetah is one of many animals threatened by hunting because of its beautiful fur.

Series editor: Sue Hadden
Series designer: Ross George

First published in 1989 by
Wayland (Publishers) Ltd
61 Western Road, Hove
East Sussex BN3 1JD, England

British Library Cataloguing in Publication Data
Penny, Malcolm
   Protecting wildlife.
   1. Wildlife conservation
   I. Title   II. Series
   639.9

ISBN 1–85210–698–0 **HARDBACK**   ISBN 0–7502–0276–9 **PAPERBACK**

Typeset by Kalligraphics Ltd, Horley, Surrey
Printed in Italy by G. Canale & C. S.p.A., Turin

Contents

It is dawn in the rainforest of Madagascar. An unearthly howl arises from among the trees. It is joined by another, then several more. Soon a chorus is ringing through the forest, making a weird harmony in the morning mist.

The singers are lemurs, a primitive group of animals related to monkeys. This particular species, called the indri, regularly greets the dawn by calling from the borders of its territory. Soon the indris will begin to feed, pulling branches to their mouths, biting off leaves and fruit.

They are tall, slender animals, covered in dense fur — brown, with silver-grey arms and legs. They

Indris survive only in a few remaining patches of Madagascar's rainforest.

move between the trees in long, athletic leaps in an upright position. When they drop to the ground to cross a clearing, they hop on both feet together, with their arms outstretched.

Some of the females have babies riding on their backs. Indri females bear their single babies only every three years: indris are very slow breeders. They are also very rare.

Some time after dawn, other voices are heard in the forest. Soon, there is the sound of chopping, and smoke drifts through the clearings. The local human inhabitants are preparing a new field to grow their crops. They have already removed the larger trees for timber and fuel; now they are felling and burning the undergrowth to clear the land. This technique is called slash and burn.

The new vegetable plot will last only for two or three years, before the soil becomes sandy and loses all its goodness. Then the people will have to move on to clear a new area of forest.

The Malagasy people brought this style of agriculture with them, when they came to Madagascar from Malaysia about 1,500 years ago. It worked well in the ancient forests that they left behind: fields which they abandoned soon recovered, going back to forest within a few years. The forests of Madagascar cannot recover in the same way, and after centuries of this method of agriculture there is little left of them — just bare, windswept hills where nothing but cattle can flourish.

The result is that the people are hungry, as the dusty soil is swept from the hills by heavy rain; and the indri, along with the other species of lemurs, are practically homeless. A few small groups of them survive in carefully protected patches of forest.

Above right *Where once the hills were covered in forest, only dry grasslands are left.*

Above *Where the Madagascan forest has been cleared, terracing helps to conserve the soil. However, crops can be grown only for a few years.*

There are similar situations all over the world, where protecting wildlife has become an urgent problem. In this book we shall examine the threats facing many animals of the world. We shall also look at the positive work that is being done to protect them from danger.

The world's rarest animals

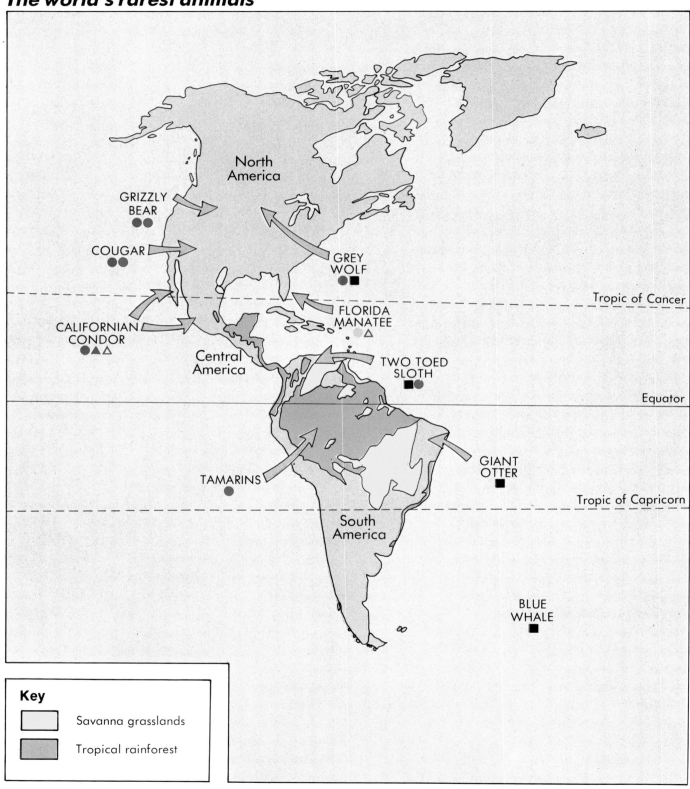

Key

Savanna grasslands

Tropical rainforest

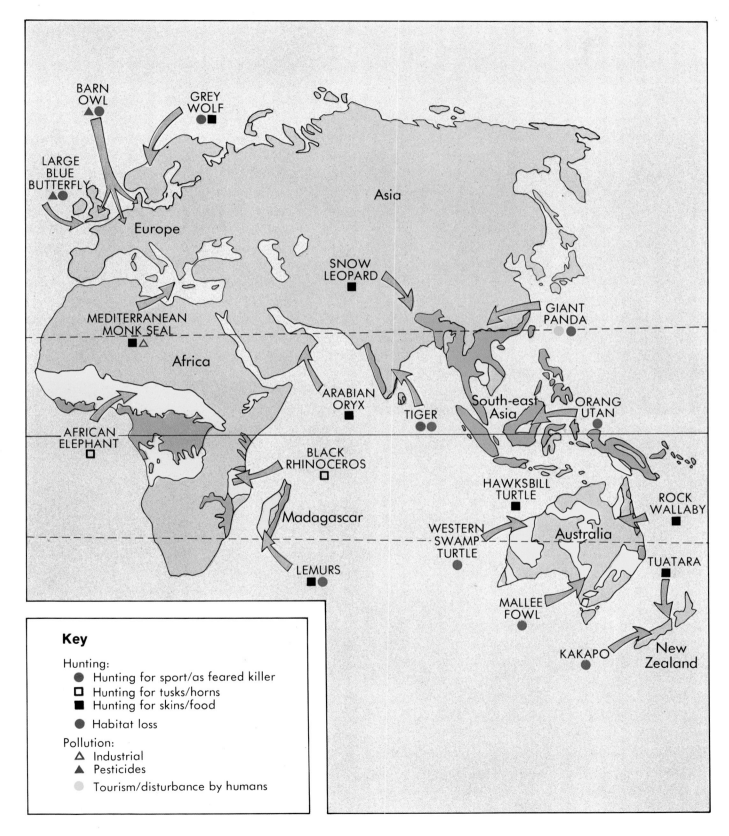

BARN OWL ▲ ●

GREY WOLF ● ■

LARGE BLUE BUTTERFLY ▲ ●

Europe

Asia

SNOW LEOPARD ■

GIANT PANDA ○ ●

MEDITERRANEAN MONK SEAL ■ △

Africa

ARABIAN ORYX ■

South-east Asia

ORANG UTAN ●

AFRICAN ELEPHANT □

TIGER ● ●

BLACK RHINOCEROS □

Madagascar

HAWKSBILL TURTLE ■

ROCK WALLABY ■

WESTERN SWAMP TURTLE ●

Australia

TUATARA ■

LEMURS ■ ●

MALLEE FOWL ●

KAKAPO ●

New Zealand

Key

Hunting:
● Hunting for sport/as feared killer
□ Hunting for tusks/horns
■ Hunting for skins/food

● Habitat loss

Pollution:
△ Industrial
▲ Pesticides

○ Tourism/disturbance by humans

beautiful birds, from humming-birds and parrots to birds of paradise. In addition, there are endless kinds of snakes and tree frogs, plus millions of insects — far too many to be identified.

When rainforests are destroyed, their unique wildlife is also doomed. For the past thirty years, rainforests have been cut down to create timber or farmland which are badly needed by the local people. However, the rate of destruction has greatly accelerated with modern technology. Already about half of the world's rainforests have been cleared. Unless effective action is taken, all our rainforests could have disappeared by early next century. With them will go their marvellous plant and animal life.

In the rainforest of Costa Rica, Central America, male golden toads gather round a pool in the breeding season.

Clouds and mist are trapped by trees and tree ferns in the rainforest of Samoa in the South Pacific ocean. In this way, the rainforest creates its own climate.

The destruction of the forests of Madagascar is typical of the loss of wildlife habitat which is going on all over the world. The areas most at risk are rainforests.

The richness of rainforests

Rainforests are moist, warm forests that thrive in tropical parts of South and Central America, Africa and South-east Asia. They have existed for tens of millions of years and contain the richest diversity of plants and animals to be found on earth. Many of the world's best-known animals live in rainforests: chimpanzees, gorillas, gibbons and most monkey species; tigers and jaguars; nocturnal bushbabies and lorises; and the world's most

Rare rainforest primates

Among the rarest primates is the golden-rumped lion tamarin, from the forests of south-east Brazil. There are less than 100 left alive in the wild, and these are now under protection in the Morro do Diabo State Reserve. However, there are twenty in a breeding colony in the Rio de Janeiro Primate Centre, where they are doing well, although it will soon be necessary to bring in some more from the wild, to prevent inbreeding.

The woolly spider monkey, also from south-east Brazil, is highly endangered. There are just 100 left, in two separate primate reserves, and perhaps twenty-five more scattered about outside. It is in greater danger than the tamarin, because it has never bred in captivity.

Below *The emperor tamarin depends on the Amazonian rainforest for survival, but its habitat is being destroyed for cattle and crop farming.*

Above *Orang-utans depend completely on the rainforest of Sumatra for food and shelter. There are less than 4,000 of them left alive.*

The orang-utan lives in the remains of the forests on the Indonesian island of Sumatra, where there are 2,000 survivors in three forest reserves, and perhaps as many again living outside the conservation areas. The chances of these wild orang-utans surviving for very long are small, because the rainforest is being destroyed at such a rapid rate.

There are two species of African gorilla in the eastern Congo and Rwanda. The mountain gorilla is the more endangered, with barely 250 survivors. The lowland gorilla may number as many as 10,000, but most people think that only half as many survive.

The dangers of erosion

A rainforest is sometimes called 'a desert covered with trees'. While the trees are standing, their roots hold the soil in place, where it is fed by the leaves and other debris falling from above. When the trees are gone, the soil has nothing to feed it. It becomes loose and sandy, and will soon be eroded, washed away by the heavy tropical rainstorms.

Erosion is one of the most serious threats to all farmland, especially in the tropics. As the rainwater carries the soil away, it forms channels which get deeper and deeper until they reach the underlying rock. The soil is carried down rivers until they reach the sea. As they flow more slowly, the rivers drop the soil in the form of silt. This chokes the river bed and increases the danger of floods.

Floods caused by deforestation in the foothills of the Himalayas make people homeless in Bangladesh, far downstream.

In the Himalayas, where the trees have been removed, terracing delays erosion, but cannot prevent it altogether. Water runs off the hillsides, carrying the soil away with it.

The most tragic example of the destruction caused by deforestation and erosion is the River Ganges. It rises in Nepal, high in the Himalayas. Where it flows through the foothills, the forests have been almost completely removed by people in need of firewood and farmland. Because of this, rainwater flows straight off the hillsides into the river, carrying a great deal of soil with it.

The river reaches the sea at the mighty Ganges Delta in Bangladesh. Here it deposits the silt from the hillsides of Nepal and India in enormous mudbanks. The soil of the Delta is very rich and fertile, and attracts many people to live there and grow crops. The mouth of the Ganges Delta was once protected by extensive mangrove forests, which helped to control the worst effects of high tides and storms at sea. However, the forests were felled to obtain building timber and firewood.

The result of these two separate acts of deforestation can be seen during the monsoon every year.

Bison once roamed the prairies of North America in vast numbers. Today only a few are left: these grazing bison are protected in Yellowstone National Park, Wyoming, USA.

Heavy rainfall rushes from the mountains towards the Delta. Monsoon winds bring high tides which invade the Delta from the sea. When these two masses of water meet, the land is flooded over an area of many square kilometres. Many people are made homeless each year. Most of the wildlife is either killed or made homeless as its habitat is destroyed by floodwater.

The loss of grasslands

Most habitat destruction arises from the need for farmland to feed the world's rapidly-increasing human population. Grasslands may be destroyed as a wildlife habitat when they are fenced off and sprayed with weedkillers, in order to raise cattle and grow corn. On the American prairies, for example, large grazing animals, such as deer and buffalo, are no longer able to move freely in search of food. Smaller animals, such as insects, and reptiles and birds that feed on them, are made homeless when the 'weeds' are killed.

Wetland plants like marsh marigolds and fritillaries have become much rarer, as most of the damp meadows in which they grow have been drained to make farmland.

Other habitats are being destroyed as well. In many parts of the world, wetlands, such as ponds and marshes, are drained to make farmland or commercial forestry plantations. Rivers are dredged, improving the drainage of the surrounding land, but at the same time destroying the habitat of creatures that live among reed-beds and in shallow streams. Land reclamation, especially beside estuaries, has made farmland out of what were once the feeding and roosting places of millions of birds.

Naturally, it is vital to humans that sufficient crops are grown to feed everyone. In the developing countries it is hard to grow enough food crops, while in many European countries and in North America there is a glut of food, leading to grain mountains and milk lakes. Many environmentalists believe that, in areas of over-production, it would be better to reduce the amount of farmland and leave some areas to become natural grassland and woodland, for wild animals.

Saving the whooping crane

Whooping cranes were always rare. Even before 1860 there were probably no more than 1,300 birds. As settlers spread across North America they disturbed the wetland places which the cranes needed to feed and rest during their migration. The wetlands were drained for agriculture, and many of the birds were shot. By 1912, there were just 88 birds left, in Texas and Louisiana. In 1941, the Louisiana population had gone, leaving 15 birds wintering on Aransas National Wildfowl Refuge in Texas. By 1977 the population of 59 had risen to 70. The crane's breeding place, in Wood Buffalo National Park, Alberta, Canada, is carefully protected. The population continues to rise, but it is still not safe. The Intracoastal Waterway, a canal for large ships, runs very close to the reserve. If there were an accident, dangerous cargoes might be spilled into the water.

In case of disaster, a new population of whooping cranes was started west of the Rocky Mountains, in Idaho. In 1977 some young whooping cranes were placed among a flock of sandhill cranes, which have a very similar migratory way of life. In 1988, the whooping cranes were still living and migrating with the sandhills, but so far they have not bred. Now there is a plan to start a third population in a similar way, in Florida.

Whooping cranes enjoy protection on Aransas National Wildfowl Refuge, Texas.

Hunting and killing

Humans have always killed other animals to eat. In a few places this is still part of everyday life: Indians in the Amazon jungles, Bushmen in Botswana, and some tribes of Inuit in North America and the USSR still hunt in the traditional way for food and raw materials.

Most people no longer have to hunt for food. Nevertheless, hunting still causes the death of many millions of wild animals every year. Many of them are killed by farmers, to protect their crops and their livestock. These 'enemies' of the farmer range in size from elephants and tigers to beetles and greenfly.

Most of the wild animals killed every year are fish. Because the demand for fish rises as the human population increases, some fisheries are in danger of running out. The fishery around

Puffins, shags and kittiwakes nest safely on remote cliffs, but their numbers in the Shetland Islands have been severely reduced by a fall in the sand eel population.

South Georgia, on the edge of the Antarctic Ocean, is the latest area to be affected by over-fishing.

Sand eels – small fish which are collected by trawling in shallow northern waters – have suffered badly from over-fishing. This has affected the large populations of birds that depend on them for food during their breeding season. Arctic terns, skuas and puffins in the Shetland Islands, off the north of Scotland, have all fallen sharply in numbers. In 1981, there were 54,000 kittiwakes in the Shetlands: by 1988, there were only a few hundred left.

The slaughter of whales

The worst example of a wild population damaged by over-hunting is the great whales. Now that most nations have abandoned whaling, there is some hope that the whale populations will eventually recover, even though there are still one or two countries which continue to kill them.

Whale meat and other whale products, such as oil, are no longer essential for anybody, except perhaps some tribes of Inuit. Commercial whaling continues because countries which have built expensive whale-chasing boats and factory ships feel that they must continue to use them until they have paid for themselves. In Japan whale meat is sold as a luxury in special restaurants, but in some countries the meat is used in the manufacture of pet foods!

Estimated whale populations

Whale species	Current numbers	Pre-whaling numbers
Blue	1,000–5,000	500,000
Humpback	1,000–3,000	300,000
Greenland right	3,800	20,000
Sperm	950,000	unknown
Fin	80,000	unknown

These figures are based on various surveys.

Whaling is now almost at an end, but has brought some species to the brink of extinction.

Hunting for sport

There is another kind of unnecessary hunting. Many people, all over the world, enjoy hunting and killing wild animals as a sport. Not very long ago, it was considered very brave and sporting to go out into the bush of Africa, or the jungles of India, to shoot lions, elephants, or tigers. Today, most people consider this type of hunting barbaric and destructive, and it has almost completely stopped. All the same, especially in North America, the shooting of wild animals is big business, with a whole industry devoted to making and selling guns and special clothing for hunters. The number of animals which may be killed is carefully controlled by the authorities.

The British population of foxes is not harmed by hunting, but this controversial blood sport still arouses many public protests.

In Yellowstone National Park, USA, some of the black bears have ventured too close to people, so they have been moved into remote areas.

Strangely enough, some kinds of sport hunting have helped the survival of wild populations. Duck-shooting in North America and Europe is a good example: the people who like to shoot ducks have made it their business to protect the places where ducks breed and feed, so that there will always be ducks for them to shoot. Fox-hunters, especially in Britain, protect foxes for the same reason.

Some animals are killed because they are dangerous. Wolves in Europe and in parts of North America are persecuted for this reason. Alligators, crocodiles, bears, mountain lions, rattlesnakes and scorpions have been killed for centuries because people are afraid of them. Now, though, some people suggest that these animals have just as much right to live as humans, but there are still many who disagree.

Victims of our vanity

The very worst kind of killing is poaching: hunting protected animals because they are worth a lot of money. Spotted cats are protected all over the world, but because there are still some people who like to wear their beautiful skins as coats, there are others who will hunt and kill the rarest leopard or cheetah to supply the market.

In the Far East, rhinoceros horn is regarded as a powerful medicine. In one Arab country, North Yemen, it is used to make the handles of the ceremonial daggers worn by every adult man. These people are prepared to pay enormous sums of money for rhino horns. A North Yemeni ceremonial dagger with a rhino horn handle can cost over $50,000. Chinese pharmacists can sell powdered or flaked horn for as much as $12,500 per kilo. Knowing this, it is easy to understand why the black rhino is now practically extinct in Africa north of the Zambezi River.

Above *Surprisingly, there are still people who think it is smart to wear the skins of spotted cats, mainly because they are very expensive.*
Until they change their minds, animals like the Asian snow leopard **(below)** *will continue to be very rare because they are hunted for their valuable coats.*

Will rhinos see the next century?

Most of the world's white rhinos now live in South Africa. This group is part of Kenya's remaining population of 30 animals.

The most endangered rhinoceros in the world is the Javan. It lives only in Udjung Kulong, a small national park on a remote Indonesian island off the tip of Java. There are no more than fifty of them left. The Sumatran rhinoceros numbers are estimated at 500-800.

The great Indian one-horned rhinoceros is actually increasing in numbers in Nepal and India, to the extent that some of them are being moved to recolonize parks where they once lived but had become extinct. There are just over 1,900 of them living today.

The white rhinoceros is relatively safe in its stronghold in South Africa, where about 4,000 are said to be breeding successfully. The black rhinoceros is said to number over 4,500, but it has a much wider range, and it is being wiped out by poachers. There are a few in a reserve in Kenya, but otherwise it has been slaughtered in all of Africa north of Zimbabwe. Even there, the surviving animals are being moved to the south of the country, away from the border with Zambia, the poachers' headquarters.

Pollution

The oldest and most common form of air pollution is smoke. Coal fires and factory chimneys fill the air with soot, blackening buildings and causing thick fog in damp weather. Now burning forests add to the pollution.

All burning fuel releases carbon dioxide. The layer of carbon dioxide in the earth's atmosphere is becoming thicker, so that it traps heat which would otherwise escape into space. This is known as the 'greenhouse effect', and it is causing the earth to become warmer. There is a danger that the polar ice-caps might start to melt, causing the level of the sea to rise. If this happens, it will alter the climate, especially the distribution of rainfall. Wildlife as well as people will be in great danger. If the climate changes abruptly, they will be unable to adapt quickly enough to survive.

The fumes from burning fossil fuels contain oxides of sulphur and nitrogen, which react with damp air to make sulphuric and nitric acids. Often, the fumes drift downwind until they come to a place where the air is damp; then they form acids, and fall as rain. Acid rain can kill fish in lakes and rivers, and has been blamed for causing the death of trees over large areas of Europe, Scandinavia, the northern USA and Canada.

The steam produced by this power station in the USA is harmless, but the fumes from the fossil fuels which it burns cause acid rain.

The atmosphere at risk

A very dangerous form of air pollution is caused by CFCs, or chlorofluorocarbons, which are used in some aerosols, refrigerators and polystyrene hamburger boxes. They drift up into the ozone layer, far above the earth's surface, and break down the ozone molecules. The ozone layer protects the earth from the harmful effects of sunlight. As it becomes thinner, more ultraviolet light will come through. This will help to raise the earth's temperature, already too high because of the greenhouse effect. It will also increase the risk of skin cancer among people. Its effect on animals and plants is hard to predict.

The radioactive fuel used in nuclear power stations gives off radiation which is extremely

The explosion at the Chernobyl nuclear power station released radiation which harmed countries far to the west. As a result, some reindeer in Norway and Lapland are still not safe to eat.

dangerous, if it escapes into the air. Even small amounts can damage human cells, causing cancer, and interfering with the development of unborn babies. The effects of radiation on wildlife are not known, but is seems most likely that they will be very similar to those on human beings. Certainly, large numbers of sheep in Britain, and reindeer in Lapland, are still radioactive following the 1986 accident at the Chernobyl nuclear power station in the USSR. This released a dangerous level of radioactivity into the atmosphere, which drifted over much of Europe.

An ocean of chemicals

Water pollution, like air pollution, is made more serious now by the numbers of people involved, and the types of harmful substances that they produce.

Oil pollution has very serious effects on wildlife. It poisons fish and seabed-dwelling animals like crabs and shellfish, and also clogs the feathers of seabirds. When the birds preen the oil from their feathers, it poisons them. Most oil-spills are accidental, but some are deliberate, for example when a tanker captain washes out his tanks at sea. Such actions are illegal, but they save time and money, and they can be carried out far at sea, out of sight of land.

The greatest threat to the marine environment is no longer oil pollution. Industrial chemicals have been invented which are far more poisonous and long-lasting. Among them is a group known as PCBs (polychlorinated biphenyls), which are used for various industrial processes. These very strong chemicals can be destroyed by burning, but because this is expensive, they are most often buried in dumps on land, or allowed to run away down rivers into the sea.

PCBs are directly poisonous, but they also weaken the immune system of many animals, so

Oil spilled into the sea kills thousands of birds every year. Only a few of them are cleaned, like these jackass penguins in South Africa.

that they become vulnerable to diseases which they would normally resist. The seal plague in the North Sea and the Baltic, first noticed in 1988, was probably made much worse because many of the seals were affected by PCBs.

Poisonous pesticides

Wild animals and plants are also harmed by pesticides and weedkillers, because these substances do not only kill the pests they are intended to, but other creatures, too. The strong chemicals contained in pesticides have harmed many insects, like butterflies, while weedkillers have killed off plants on which their caterpillars feed.

Pesticides can harm many animals because they are passed along the food chain. For example, a field mouse may eat grains of wheat treated with pesticide. The pesticide chemicals are not used up, but stored in the mouse's body. If the mouse is caught by a barn owl, the harmful chemicals will be passed on to the owl. Since barn owls catch many mice, they will in time receive a poisonous dose of pesticides. The accumulated chemicals harm their eggs and the babies that hatch from them.

From what you have read, you can see that humans have polluted the air, the land and the water, causing much harm to animals and plants.

Organizations like Greenpeace keep pollution in the news by their daring demonstrations.

Harvest mice flourish in fields of wheat. They suffered in the past from the use of pesticides, and from modern harvesting machinery, which cuts the crop very close to the ground and destroys their nests. Now there are signs that their population is recovering.

The idea of protecting large areas of wild land was first put into practice in the USA in 1872, when Yellowstone National Park was opened. Since then, national parks have been founded in almost every country in the world.

When Yellowstone was founded, wildlife in the Rocky Mountains was not in any danger. The park was set up to protect the extraordinary landscape of geysers and sulphur springs, so that Americans could marvel at it for ever. The fact that it was full of wildlife, including buffalo, grizzly bears and herds of elk, was a secondary consideration.

Ibex were one of the first animals to be given protection in a national park. Gran Paradiso National Park in Italy not only protects ibex, but also provides a safe home for many other alpine animals and plants.

Later, national parks were established to protect particular species of animal, usually from over-hunting. The first of these was in Italy, when in 1922 the King gave his hunting preserve at Gran Paradiso to the nation, to protect the alpine ibex. Since then, most parks have been established to protect the whole environment, including all its animals and plants.

Some people say that national parks are a waste of space, especially in countries where there is a land shortage. However, parks attract tourists, who bring much-needed money into the country from overseas. Unless a country protects some big game animals, there will be nothing for the tourists to see. However, many people believe it is important to save animals because they too have a right to live — not just because they are interesting to look at.

Saving the tiger

For many people the tiger is the world's most majestic animal. However, the tiger was hunted for sport, and much of its forest habitat was lost to farmland, until its numbers were drastically reduced. By the early 1970s the World Wide Fund for Nature devised an action plan to save the tiger from extinction. Under the name Project Tiger, the Indian government worked with WWF to create eight reserves where the tigers would be protected from hunters. The reserves cover an area of 26,000 km^2 and offer a safe home to many other animals.

The project has been highly successful and the tiger population doubled from under 2,000 in 1972 to over 4,000 in 1983. Now the future of this superb animal seems assured.

The future of national parks

For a national park to be a success, there must be a balance between the needs of the local people and those of the animals. A good example is Royal Chitwan National Park, in Nepal. It is partly forest, and partly elephant grass over 2m tall. Tigers and one-horned rhinoceroses live there, together with two different species of crocodile. However, the park is surrounded by villages, whose people need firewood from the forest and grass from the plain, to build houses and feed cattle.

To save arguments, the local people are allowed into the Park at certain times of year to collect grass. The Park staff collect dead wood from the forest, and driftwood from the rivers, for the villagers to use as fuel. The villagers are encouraged to plant 'firewood forests' around the edge of the Park, to provide a renewable fuel supply. The Park is safe, and the people no longer feel that it is taking land which they need.

The millions of water birds which live in the Everglades National Park include roseate spoonbills, great egrets and tricoloured herons.

One of the oldest and largest national parks in the USA, the Florida Everglades, is suffering from a similar conflict. The park relies on a steady flow of clean water from the north. Unfortunately, the water is also needed for agriculture. More and more people are moving to Florida and it is necessary to drain land to build houses, and to provide people with water. This drainage removes some of the water from the edges of the park. The water which comes from the farmland is often polluted with fertilizer. This polluted water enters the tidal swamps, causing an excessive growth of some green algae. Eventually the algae would cover the water, removing all oxygen from it. If the problem is not solved soon, the Everglades will be lost, with all its wonderful scenery, and the millions of superb birds, snakes and alligators that live there.

Royal Chitwan National Park in Nepal protects tigers and one-horned rhinoceroses. Visitors ride elephants to view the wildlife.

The Everglades is considered so important that it has been declared a World Heritage Site, to be looked after by everybody. Some other World Heritage Sites are Mount Everest, the Grand Canyon, USA, the Serengeti in Africa, and Lake Ichkeul in Tunisia, which is an important wetland used by migrant birds.

National parks are important to the whole world, because they will be the only way for future generations to know what the world looked like before farmland and cities took over. Many of them are also the last home of animals which used to be common.

In Africa, the only hope for the black rhinoceros is to be protected in national parks, with armed guards to keep the poachers away, until people stop buying rhinoceros horn. Biologists have discovered ways of making rhinoceroses breed more quickly, by adjusting the numbers in each park. People who object to this say that it is turning Africa into a vast zoo. However, if wild animals are to survive at all, zoos may have an important part to play.

A black rhinoceros mother and her calf have been rescued from farmland, transported by lorry, and released into Etosha National Park, Namibia. Such efforts are often necessary to protect endangered rhinoceroses from poachers, who hunt them for their horns.

Saving animals in zoos

Until recently, a zoo (or zoological garden, to use the full name) was a place to visit with the family, to admire the exotic animals as they paced around their cages, and perhaps to have a ride on a camel or an elephant. The first zoo was established in London, in the grounds of the Zoological Society at Regent's Park. It was followed by others in most countries in the world. Some, such as the Bronx Zoo in New York, are enormous, with hundreds of rare animals for people to see.

Gradually the organizers of zoos tried to make the enclosures more realistic, and included more information on notices so that their visitors would learn something about the animals, as well as staring at them in awe. However, for a long time the animals in zoos were all captured from the wild, and very rarely bred in captivity. Such old-fashioned zoos still exist, although they are getting fewer, as more and more countries ban the capture of wild animals.

Zoos such as the one in Hamburg, West Germany, are important reservoirs of rare animals. Increasingly, zoos aim to raise public awareness of the threats facing the world's wildlife.

The world breeding herd of Arabian oryx at Phoenix, Arizona, was the means of saving this beautiful species from extinction.

The changing role of zoos

Zoos still have an important part to play in letting people have a close look at animals which they will probably never see in the wild. However, the most important function of a modern zoo is as a reservoir of rare animals, which can be bred in captivity. This provides stock for other zoos, so that no more wild animals need to be captured, and also provides animals which can be released into their original habitat, when it is safe to do so. Two very successful early examples of this type of work involved the Arabian oryx and the Hawaiian goose.

The Arabian oryx was hunted by men in cars and jeeps, using automatic rifles, until it became extinct in the wild in 1972. A charitable British organization called the Flora and Fauna Preservation Society arranged to collect all the surviving oryx together, from zoos and private collections, to establish a captive breeding herd in Phoenix, Arizona, USA. The experiment was successful, and in 1982 animals bred from the herd in the USA were released into part of their original habitat, in Oman. The animals were released only after the local government had passed laws to protect the oryx from hunting. Today, the wild herd is breeding successfully in Oman.

By 1978, nearly 500 nenes had been released into protected areas on the islands of Maui and Hawaii. Today, there are at least 750 nenes living in the wild, and well over a thousand living and breeding in captivity. Like the Arabian oryx, the nene now survives in its original habitat only because of the efforts of humans.

While the nenes were being bred, wild birds were brought into the captive flocks from time to time, to prevent inbreeding which made the birds infertile. Zoos now work in the same way. Instead of breeding from the same small group of animals all the time, they exchange animals between themselves, keeping track of the breeding population of many rare species by means of a 'stud book' or family tree. The animals are kept as a breeding population ready for the time when they might be released safely into the wild.

Left *Captive breeding may be the only chance of survival for some rare animals. Modern techniques have made it possible to increase the breeding rate: here a female eland has given birth to a baby bongo, a rare African species of bushbuck. The bongo was removed from its natural mother as an embryo, and transplanted into the eland.*

The Hawaiian goose, or nene, was similarly endangered in the Hawaiian islands where it lived. Its habitat had been destroyed by cattle and goats, and the geese were threatened by predators such as pigs, dogs, cats and mongooses, which had been brought to the islands and allowed to run wild. The nene evolved in an environment where it had no predators, so it was easy to catch. By 1951, there were less than thirty birds left. Three, two females and a male, were sent to the Wildfowl Trust, in Gloucestershire, England, and others were taken into captivity in Hawaii, in the hope that they would breed.

Right *Hawaiian geese were saved from extinction at the Wildfowl Trust, Slimbridge, England.*

Rainforest monkeys in captivity

Some monkeys settle down well in captivity, and there are breeding populations of them in a number of zoos. Some examples are:

Goeldi's marmoset, a small monkey of the Brazilian rainforest. It breeds successfully in Jersey Zoo, Great Britain, and Brookfield Zoo in Chicago, USA. Of 100 at present held captive, 61 were bred in the zoos where they live.

Red-backed squirrel monkey, from Panama and Costa Rica. There are 55 held in eight different zoos. Twelve of them are captive-bred.

Brown howler monkey. There is a captive breeding population of this monkey in the Primate Centre at Rio de Janeiro, Brazil.

At Looe, in Cornwall, England, woolly monkeys breed in captivity. By seeing them at close quarters, people become sympathetic to their plight in the wild, and may lend their support to the campaign to save the rainforests.

Woolly monkey, from north-western South America. It is the first monkey to disappear when humans encroach on its forest home, and consequently it has attracted a lot of sympathy over the years. There are 226 woolly monkeys held captive in 50 different zoos.

Of this population, 58 have been bred in captivity.

The ultimate success of these captive breeding programmes depends on whether large areas of rainforest can be made safe enough for the monkeys to be released into the wild.

Changing our behaviour

We have already seen that the best hope for the black rhino is that people should change their beliefs about the value of its horn, so that the trade in daggers and medicines collapses. Many other changes in beliefs and behaviour will be necessary if the natural world is to survive for much longer.

The scheme to persuade villagers in Nepal to plant trees for firewood is being carried out, not only on the plains near Chitwan National Park, but also in the foothills of the Himalayas. As more trees are planted there, the land will become more stable, instead of being washed away down the rivers, and there will be less danger of flooding in faraway Bangladesh.

Pollution can be reduced as well, for example by discouraging people from using pesticides and artificial fertilizers on farmland. Today a growing number of people are realizing that soil can be enriched, and pests controlled, by organic methods. Such methods are less suited to large-scale farming, but farmers can use less harmful chemicals.

The use of CFCs has already been greatly reduced, and there are moves to ban the manufacture and use of most of the PCBs, which have caused so much damage to the environment in the short time since they were invented.

Scientists are working hard to find other ways of providing energy. 'Alternative energy sources', as they are called, include wind and water power, and solar energy. Finding alternative energy sources is important for two reasons: they will reduce the pollution from burning fossil fuels, and they will postpone the time when the fossil fuels are used up.

Introduced plants such as brambles grew too well in New Zealand. Herbicide sprayed from a helicopter is a desperate attempt to control them.

Saving the rainforests

The destruction of rainforests can also be reduced, by changing the way in which people clear the land, and by using the land better when it has been cleared. The main problem with rainforest soil is that it is very soft, made up of leaves which have fallen over thousands of years. If the trees are cleared with heavy machinery, this fragile soil is squashed flat. It quickly becomes waterlogged, and bad for growing plants. If the trees are cleared by people on foot, the soil survives much better.

To help the forests and their animals to survive, it would be better if the clearings were much

This cleared patch of Brazilian rainforest was once the home of the rare golden lion tamarin.

smaller, leaving 'corridors' of forest between them. The animals would still have somewhere to live, and the trees would still be there to produce seeds. Thus the clearings would recover more quickly when the soil was no longer suitable for growing crops.

There are schemes to slow down the destruction of rainforests in countries as far apart as Mexico and Madagascar, but at present they are on rather a small scale. It is important that more areas of rainforest be protected, while there are still some worthwhile areas of forest left.

Killing for the sake of tradition

In many places in the Mediterranean, migrating songbirds are killed in enormous numbers in spring and autumn. Although the people eat the birds, they cannot be said to be essential food. As a result of this hunting, many of the birds which breed in Europe and spend the winter in Africa are becoming rare.

The Californian Condor: doomed like the dodo?

The Californian condor is a very long-lived bird, and very slow to breed, about once every three years. Its numbers were reduced by shooting, trapping, poisoning and egg-collecting, until in 1977 there were less than 40 birds left alive. By 1988 the numbers were down to 20, and it seems inevitable that the species will soon become extinct. There is a small experimental captive breeding programme, but so far it has met with no success. The condor is a tragic example of a bird which has become so rare that there are too few left in the wild to breed successfully.

You might think that once the hunters understood the harm that they are doing, they would stop their spring and autumn hunting, but it is not that easy. The hunt is an old tradition, dating back to the time when the tiny amount of food that each bird provided was a rare treat to a hungry population. Now the people carry on the tradition for its own sake, and do not like to be told that they ought to give it up.

In a similar tradition, people in the Scandinavian Faroe Islands slaughter small whales, in spite of protests from other countries. Each year they kill thousands of pilot whales and white-sided dolphins. The Faroese people do not need the meat; most of it ends up on rubbish dumps, after each family has had a celebration meal.

There are hunting traditions all over the world, from kangaroo-killing in Australia to rattlesnake-hunting in Texas. One day, a generation may grow up which realizes that these traditional practices cause more damage than they are worth.

Traditional whale-hunting in the Faroe Islands continues in spite of international protests at the cruelty and wastage of the slaughter. These pilot whales have been driven into a bay and hacked to death.

The main threat to wildlife habitat comes from the ever-increasing human population, and its constant demand for housing, farms, and roads, all of which require vast areas of land.

The greatest threat to wildlife

The main problem threatening wildlife in the world today is the rapid growth of the human population. This, too, is largely a matter of behaviour and tradition. In the past, most of the children born to a family became ill and died before they grew up. Therefore it made sense to have as many children as possible, so that at least a few would survive to help their parents. With modern medicine, many more children survive, and such large families are not necessary. Birth control is now effective and much simpler than in the past. However, there are serious religious and political problems in the way of limiting the growth of the human population. Such problems will have to be solved before there is any real hope of controlling the human population and so allowing the survival of the natural world.

Illegally trapped chimpanzees are sold for use in medical research. Some of them are deliberately infected with the AIDS virus, to help in the search for a cure for humans.

A brighter future?

Although the early chapters of this book contain a lot of bad news, there is some good news which should not be ignored. As we have seen, there are many organizations working to protect the natural world, and they have had a good deal of success. We have already seen how two unofficial charities managed to save the Arabian oryx and the Hawaiian nene.

Conservation in action

The largest official conservation organization is the International Union for the Conservation of Nature and Natural Resources (IUCN). With the advice of experts from all over the world, IUCN spends thousands of millions of dollars every year on conservation. Part of its funds come from the World Wide Fund for Nature (WWF), which itself has branches in twenty-three countries, and

conservation schemes in nearly 100 countries.

Both organizations are involved in the Convention on International Trade in Endangered Species (CITES), which controls the movements of animals and animal products, from cage birds and lizards to rhino horn and ivory. As more and more countries join the Convention (there were ninety-six members in 1988), there are signs that this destructive trade will soon come to an end.

The most successful conservation efforts work at a local level, by convincing people who live among the endangered animals and habitats that they can do something to help. Here are two success stories, both to do with butterflies.

Plumes from birds of paradise were used by the people of Papua New Guinea in their traditional dress. Now, though, the people protect these beautiful birds for visitors to see.

An Australian conservation success story

Australia's rarest possum, the mountain pygmy possum, has been saved from extinction by an ingenious plan developed by WWF Australia. This tiny creature only lives on Mount Higginbotham in Victoria, but the development of a ski resort there put its future in jeopardy.

Male and female mountain pygmy possums live separately for most of the year, only meeting during the breeding season. The construction of an Alpine Tourist Road had permanently separated the males from the females, preventing them from breeding. Unless they could mate, these rare possums would become extinct. Those male possums who tried to cross the busy road were killed by fast cars.

Fortunately, WWF stepped in and suggested that a tunnel be built under the road, so allowing the mountain pygmy possums to meet and breed. The idea was approved by the Victorian Government and the Alpine Sports Commission and so the tunnel was built, despite its cost of 34,000 Australian dollars. It has been an immediate success and now there is no danger of these rare possums dying out.

In New Guinea, the local people used to trap birds of paradise so that they could sell their feathers. They also caught large rainforest butterflies to make their wings into ornaments and pictures. Nowadays, they protect the birds for visitors to watch, from special hides which they have built. When the visitors leave, they can buy the butterfly ornaments, but they are no longer made from wild butterflies. The villagers breed butterflies for the purpose, in enclosures at the edge of protected areas of rainforest where their food plants grow. The wild butterfly population is no longer threatened.

Monarch butterflies migrate from all over North America to spend the winter in pine forests in the mountains of Mexico. The local people there had been felling the trees where the butterflies roosted, to make clearings where they could grow crops and raise cattle. Today, the people who used to chop down the trees have realized that they have a greater value to people if they leave them standing. Visitors come from all over the world to see the astonishing sight of millions of butterflies in the mountain forests. The villagers sell them snacks and souvenirs.

At Pacific Grove, California, children join in a special parade to mark the day when the migrating monarch butterflies return.

Both these stories show the importance of tourism. It has become easy for people to travel to far-away places for holidays, and every year more people save up for a special journey. As well as providing money for the national parks and the countries which they visit, all these travellers act as witnesses to what is going on, reporting back to their home countries, and enticing more travellers to go to the best places. Their reports may also encourage other people to give money to WWF, and similar organizations, which start these schemes and help to keep them going.

Kakapos are a kind of flightless parrot found only in New Zealand. They have become very rare due to destruction of their habitat, and now there are schemes to conserve them. In the photograph New Zealand Wildlife Service officers feed a captured kakapo with liquid nectar during a study of the small remaining population.

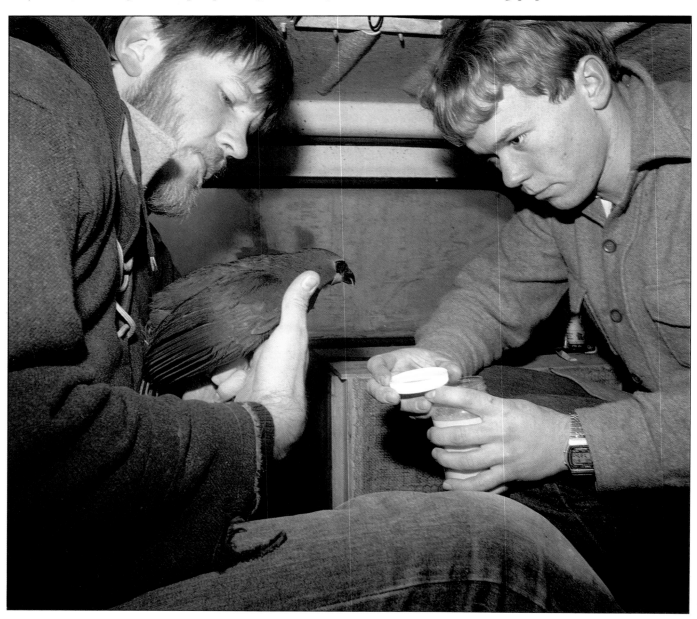

A pair of Large Blue butterflies on their foodplant, wild thyme.

How a butterfly was saved from extinction

The Large Blue is a beautiful European butterfly with a special life cycle. Its caterpillars need an insect partner to help them survive – a particular species of ant. A colony of these ants 'kidnaps' the Large Blue caterpillar and takes it back to their nest, where they look after it until it pupates and eventually leaves them as an adult butterfly. Why do the ants do this? They love to feed on a honey-like secretion produced by the caterpillar.

The Large Blue has become rarer throughout Europe because of changes in farming practices and the use of pesticides. In 1979 it became extinct in Britain. Fortunately it has been saved by an enterprising conservation scheme, run jointly by the Nature Conservancy Council, the Institute of Terrestrial Ecology and the World Wide Fund for Nature.

In August 1986 over 200 caterpillars were brought to Britain from a Swedish Large Blue colony. They were released at a secret site in south-west Britain. In 1988, some 4,500 eggs were laid by the introduced butterflies. It is estimated that their numbers will grow over a period of several years to make a British population of about 9,000.

To guarantee the future survival of the Large Blue, conservation groups grow its food plant, wild thyme, in its breeding area and also ensure that its ant partner is doing well.

Hope for the lemurs?

There are many other pieces of good news to set against the bad we so often hear. One which should not be left out is the news from Madagascar, where this book began.

All the island's lemurs are threatened by forest destruction, and by hunting, despite being protected by law. One species, the aye-aye, had to be removed from Madagascar to ensure its survival. In 1966, nine aye-ayes were moved from the mainland to the quieter island of Nosy Mangabe, which was declared a special reserve. There is some evidence that the small aye-aye population is slowly increasing on Nosy Mangabe, and may number about fifty.

An aye aye, the rarest lemur, can bite into green coconuts to drink the juice.

On Madagascar itself the situation is still very serious, but at last the Malagasy people are finding ways to do something about it. A conference in 1970, between the government of Madagascar, IUCN, WWF and other interested organizations, led to the development of a national plan for conservation. The plan eventually became official in 1984. It was slow to arrive, but it already shows signs of working well.

Areas of the remaining forest are now preserved, and surrounded by 'buffer zones' where the forest is being allowed to grow back. This protects the reserves, where lemurs survive, from the effects of slash and burn agriculture.

For some of Madagascar's lemurs, for example the broad-nosed gentle lemur, it may be too late. For the species which survive, there is a good chance that they will now be safe, along with all the other wildlife in the forest reserves.

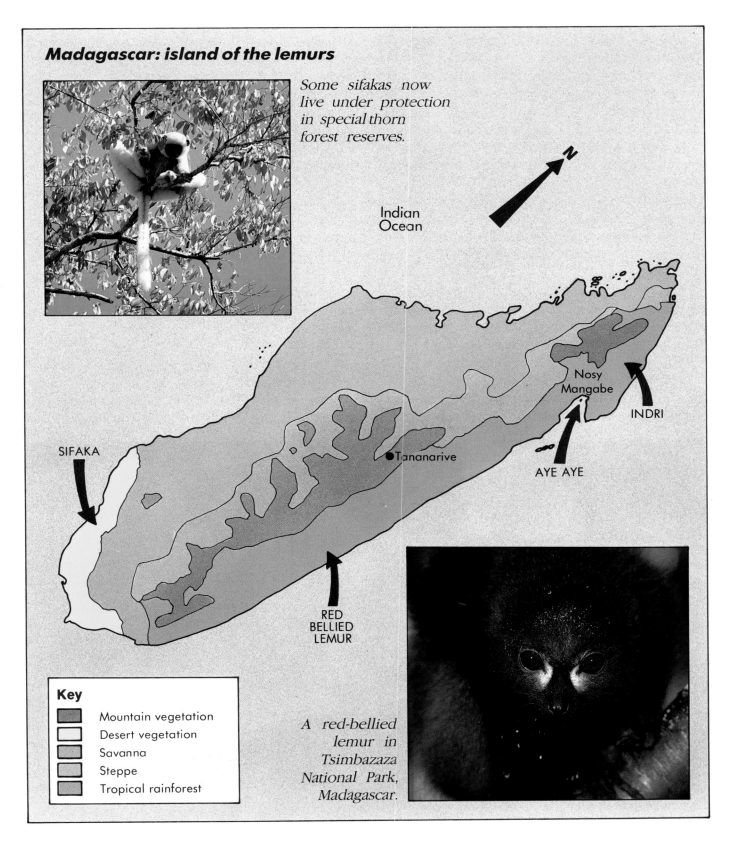

Madagascar: island of the lemurs

Some sifakas now live under protection in special thorn forest reserves.

Indian Ocean

N

Nosy Mangabe

INDRI

AYE AYE

•Tananarive

SIFAKA

RED BELLIED LEMUR

Key
- Mountain vegetation
- Desert vegetation
- Savanna
- Steppe
- Tropical rainforest

A red-bellied lemur in Tsimbazaza National Park, Madagascar.

There are many organizations which exist to safeguard the environment. You will find a list of some of them at the back of this book. By joining, and supporting the local group, you can let the authorities know that you, too, are concerned with what is happening to the natural world.

The World Wide Fund for Nature (WWF) has many different projects to protect wildlife and special habitats all over the world. WWF also publishes the Conservation Yearbook, containing a report of its activities. The enormous scope of WWF's operations all over the world encourages people to give as much as they can to keep the work going.

Collecting bird's eggs is now illegal in many countries, as the result of campaigns by the Royal Society for the Protection of Birds, and the International Council for Bird Preservation.

When the seals in the North Sea began to die of a virus during 1988, the Royal Society for the Prevention of Cruelty to Animals joined forces with Greenpeace to set up a centre where sick seals could be treated. Their action helped a number of seals, and earned useful publicity. Soon everyone who saw a newspaper knew that the disease was probably made worse by pollution in the North Sea. Greenpeace in particular is campaigning to reduce pollution of many kinds.

You can join any of these organizations, to help to spread their message. However, conservation does not have to be a public matter: it can be personal too.

On a walk in the country, for example, a good motto is 'Look, don't touch'. In some nature reserves there is a sign which says 'Take only photographs, leave only footprints'. If everyone followed this advice, there would be much less damage to the plants and animals which make the countryside such a marvellous place.

A baby seal being treated at the Seal Orphanage at Pieterburen in Holland. The outbreak of seal distemper helped to draw people's attention to the pollution in the North Sea.

Making room for wildlife

If you have a garden, you can make your own nature reserve. To encourage butterflies, for example, you could plant a shrub called Buddleia or 'butterfly bush'. It has sweet-scented flower spikes which produce lots of nectar. Butterflies love it.

You can encourage many butterflies to breed, too, by letting nettles grow. Nettles are among the best plants for insects. Over forty different species of insect depend on them, including the caterpillars of five species of butterfly: Comma, Small Tortoiseshell, Red Admiral, Peacock and Painted Lady. When the nettles become a nuisance, they should be cut down, not sprayed with weedkiller. The stems and leaves are rich in natural nitrogen, and make excellent compost.

In the countryside, ditches and ponds are often drained, or become polluted by fertilizers and weedkillers. By creating a pond in your garden, you can provide an alternative home for frogs and many freshwater insects, including beautiful dragonflies.

You can also help wild birds in winter. Bird-feeders and bird-baths are especially valuable to birds in winter, when food is scarce and water may be frozen. Once the birds know that food and water are available in your garden, or on the balcony of your flat, many different species may come to feed there. When small birds visit a garden in winter, they help to control pests by eating the eggs of aphids that lie under the bark of trees.

Protecting wildlife and wild places is the responsibility of each one of us. If we successfully conserve the rich wildlife we still have now, the world will be a much nicer place in the future. Listed overleaf are some practical ways of helping to look after wildlife. How can you help to protect our wildlife for the future?

In the suburbs of Australian towns, where they are not under pressure from farmers, grey kangaroos can become very tame.

Eight steps to protecting wildlife

- Tell people why it is harmful to use insecticides and weedkillers.

- Avoid using aerosols that contain CFCs. Do not accept goods, such as hamburgers, if they are wrapped in polystyrene packaging that contains CFCs.

- Learn as much about your local wildlife as you can. Try to visit a local nature reserve, or find out if there is an area near you where you can see plenty of wildlife.

- Join a conservation organization and keep up to date with its wildlife protection schemes.

- You may be particularly interested in birds, or wild flowers, or insects. Develop your interest as much as possible, using guidebooks to help you to find and identify animals and plants.

- Create a wildlife corner in your garden, or ask if you can do this in your school garden.

- Write to your local newspaper or political representative if you are worried that a certain plant or animal is threatened by human activities.

- Tell your friends why it is important to protect wildlife. Remember that all creatures have a right to live, even the spider in your bath!

Making a wildlife garden

You can enjoy growing wild flowers in your garden, and encourage wildlife. Butterflies love thistle flowers, while birds such as goldfinches enjoy eating the seed heads. Bees like clover, poppies, and bluebells.

You can obtain wild flower seed from most garden shops. Set aside a flower border and sow the seed there. Let other 'weeds', especially nettles and grasses, grow with your wild flowers. When they have finished flowering, allow them to set seed for next year. If you make a pile of leaves in the autumn, a small wild animal may hibernate there during the winter.

Glossary

Acid rain Rainwater containing waste gases which have made it more acid than normal.

Agriculture The process of cultivating land so that it produces food.

Algae (singular: alga) Mostly single-celled plants which live in water.

Conservation Ensuring the survival of plants and animals in their natural habitat.

Deforestation Removing trees from the land.

Endangered Reduced in numbers so that the species is likely to die out.

Erosion The process in which soil is washed away by water or blown away by wind.

Estuary The wide, shallow part of a river where it reaches the sea.

Evolved Developed over a long period of time.

Extinction The point at which all the members of a species have died out.

Fertilizers Natural or artificial substances added to soil to improve its ability to support crops.

Food chain A natural 'chain' in which one animal eats another, so passing energy down the 'chain'.

Fossil fuels Oil, gas, and coal are all fossil fuels.

'Greenhouse' effect Changes in the earth's atmosphere which reduce the normal escape of heat into space, so warming the earth's climate.

Habitat The natural home of an animal or plant, for example, woodland, grassland and desert.

Inbreeding Where too few male and female animals breed, which increases the chance of illness among new-born animals.

Infertile Unable to breed successfully.

Irrigation Supplying water to farmland.

Land reclamation Draining or filling areas of shallow water, to increase the area of dry land.

Migrate To move from one part of the world to another as the seasons change.

Monsoon A seasonal wind in South-east Asia which often brings heavy rain.

Nocturnal Active at night.

Organic A natural method of farming that does not use chemical fertilizers and pesticides.

PCBs (polychlorinated biphenyls). Chemicals used for cleaning machinery or tanning leather.

Pesticides Chemicals used for killing insects which attack crops.

Pollution The release into the environment of harmful substances which damage living things.

Primates The group of mammals including monkeys, apes and baboons.

Pupate To change from a caterpillar into a cocoon.

Radiation The transfer of energy by means of rays or particles. Nuclear radiation is energy which comes from the breakdown of atoms.

Radioactive Producing nuclear radiation.

Virus A tiny living organism which can cause disease.

Further reading

Allaby, Michael, *Ecology Facts* (Hamlyn, 1986)

Baines, John, *Acid Rain* (Wayland, 1989)

Banks, Martin, *Conserving Rainforests* (Wayland, 1989)

Day, David, *The Whale War* (Routledge and Kegan Paul, 1987)

Durrell, Lee, *The State of the Ark* (Bodley Head, 1986)

McCormick, John, *Acid Rain* (Franklin Watts, 1985)

Penny, Malcolm, *Endangered Animals* (Wayland, 1988)

Penny, Malcolm, *Rhinos; Endangered Species* (Christopher Helm, 1987)

Penny, Malcolm, *Pollution and Conservation* (Wayland, 1988)

Useful addresses

Acid Rain Information Centre
Department of Environmental and Geographic Studies
Manchester Polytechnic
Chester Street
Manchester M1 5GD
England

Acid Rain Information Clearing House
Centre for Environmental Information Inc.
33 S. Washington Street
Rochester NY 14608
USA

Australian Association for Environmental Education
GPO Box 112
Canberra ACT 2601
Australia

Environment and Conservation Organizations of New Zealand (ECO)
P.O. Box 11057
Wellington
New Zealand

Fauna and Flora Preservation Society
79-83 North Street
Brighton BN1 1ZA
England

Friends of the Earth
26-28 Underwood Street
London N1 7JQ
England

Friends of the Earth (Australia)
National Liaison Office
366 Smith Street
Collingwood
Victoria 3065

Friends of the Earth (Canada)
Suite 53 54
Queen Street
Ottawa KP5CS

Friends of the Earth (NZ)
Nagal House
Courthouse Lane
PO Box 39/065
Auckland West

Greenpeace (UK)
30-31 Islington Green
London N1 8XE

Greenpeace (USA)
1611 Connecticut Avenue N.W.
Washington DC2009

Greenpeace (Australia)
310 Angas Street
Adelaide 5000

Greenpeace (Canada)
2623 West 4th Avenue
Vancouver BCV6K 1P8

Watch
22 The Green
Nettleham
Lincs LN2 2NR
England

World Wide Fund for Nature
WWF Information and Education Division
1196 Gland
Switzerland

Index

Picture acknowledgements

The publishers would like to thank the following for allowing their photographs to be reproduced in this book: Bryan and Cherry Alexander 21; Ardea London Ltd 40 (Liz and Tony Bomford); Bruce Coleman Ltd 4 and 41 below (O. Langrand), 8 below and 33 (L.C. Marigo), 9 above and 22 (Gerald Cubitt), 9 below (Dieter and Mary Plage), 11, 17 and 34 (Jeff Foott), 13 (Joy Langsbury), 14 (John Markham), 19 (Christian Zuber), 20 (Robert Carr), 26 above (Erwin and Peggy Bauer), 28 (Francisco Futil), 29 (Jen and Des Bartlett), 30 below (Gordon Langsbury), 35 above (Bruce Coleman), 35 below (Helmut Albrecht), 36 (Huli Wigmen); Environmental Investigation Agency 34 (Dave Currey); Frank Lane 30 above (Ron Austing), 31 (Frank W Lane); Greenpeace 23 below (Morgan), 42 (Dorreboom); ICCE 6 (Sue Wells), 8 above (John Mackinnon); Oxford Scientific Films 5 above and 41 above (Mark Pidgeon), 5 below (David Curl), 7 (Michael Fogden), 16 (Anna Walsh), 18 below (Michael Dick), 19 (Mike Birkhead), 23 (Sean Morris); Rex Features 10; Survival Anglia Ltd 12 and 37 (Jeff Foott), 26 below (Dieter Plage), 27 (Jen and Des Bartlett), 38 (Annie Price) 39 (Dennis Green); ZEFA 15 (K. Scholz), 24, 43 (P. Blok)
The illustrations are by Marilyn Clay.